RENÉE JONES

Mama Ain't Teach Me That

A True Story About Me and the Hidden Story About You

Mama Ain't Teach Me That
Copyright © 2011 Renée Jones

All Rights Reserved.

No part of this publication may be reproduced, stored in a retrieval system, or transmitted in any form or by any means – electronic, mechanical, photocopying, recording, or otherwise – without the written permission of the author or publisher. The only exception is brief quotations in printed reviews.

First published by Faith Books & MORE
978-0-9846507-4-3

Printed in the United States of America.

This book is printed on acid-free paper.

3255 Lawrenceville-Suwanee Rd.
Suite P250
Suwanee, GA 30024
publishing@faithbooksandmore.com
www.faithbooksandmore.com

Table of Contents

Locked in a Box 1

A Lap Today, a Slap Tomorrow 9

The Protector 13

Who Could I Talk to Now 17

Please Stop the Pain 21

In the Name of Love 27

The Key to My Jail 33

Freedom Isn't Free 37

A Sandwich Bag 41

Left to Find a Husband 47

Twenty Dollar High 51

I Took Me with Me 55

The Start of the New Life 59

She Was Not Joking 63

You Will Find Haters 69

He Loves Me 73

Epilogue 77

Letters from Loved Ones 81

Resources 86

About the Author 90

Dedication

I dedicate this book to ALL the survivors of abuse.

Dear Mom,

I have felt so much pain during the days, months and year that I worked on this book. I did it to help others just like me, not to hurt you at all. I love you more today than I ever did.

Working through my life, I have learned you worked with what you had, but I CAN SAY WE NEVER MISSED A MEAL and HAD WONDERFUL CHRISTMASES. For that, I thank you.

Today I can call on you and you listen. For that, I thank you.

Love your daughter,
Renée S. Jones

Acknowledgements

Thank you to my book reviewers Yvette Barr, Lisa Pierce and Nicole Smith for providing me with feedback.

The Serenity Prayer by Reinhold Niebuhr

God grant me the serenity
to accept the things I cannot change;
courage to change the things I can;
and wisdom to know the difference.

Living one day at a time;
Enjoying one moment at a time;
Accepting hardships as the pathway to peace;
Taking, as He did, this sinful world
as it is, not as I would have it;
Trusting that He will make all things right
if I surrender to His Will;
That I may be reasonably happy in this life
and supremely happy with Him
Forever in the next.
Amen.

PREFACE

On a daily basis, I have to treat my mental health issue. For me, the best way to keep a balance is to pray, eat healthily, exercise, take the medication as prescribed by my doctor and step out myself to help others.

In this book, you will learn the truth about me and perhaps the hidden truth about you.

As a Chemical Dependency Counselor Assistant working on my bachelor's degree with the goal of licensed by 2012/2013, I continue to work in the field, a way to better my education on these diseases. In the groups, I facilitate, it is important for me to keep it interesting for my clients. The groups really belong to them and they must learn and understand treatment and recovery. One of the groups I enjoy is the resentment group. I use a large potato in this group. First, we talk about resentments. We all have them. We can say we do not, but we do. It might be the post office line took too long, or the mail carrier is late. Resentments are in us. If only for a day, they are there. We share about them. We pick one person, place or thing and write that name on the potato. I ask the clients to carry that potato around with them in treatment for about four hours. At the next group meeting, we talk about how hard it was holding onto the potato. In addition, how it was in the way of our day.

At the end of the group we ask ourselves, will it be better for me to let go of all the stuff I am carrying around or to hold onto that dead weight? The group chooses to let go.

I have committed my life to helping others. A promise I made to my God and to myself, a promise to keep.

Can you imagine living in a house with twelve people and feeling alone? When you have sisters and brothers, stepsisters and stepbrothers, all living together in a two-bedroom house you are seldom actually alone. Therefore, it may seem unusual to feel alone. If you know that feeling, you know there are many things we will never tell, things such as fantasizing at an early age, not understanding what love is, or dealing with the pain and fear of abuse. Later finding out that as a result, suffering some mental health issues. Nevertheless, to keep a promise I made to God, in this book I share some of the things I have gone through. I hope they will make a difference in your life.

People always say, if you want HELP, ask for it, but they never tell you who to ask. It seems I usually asked the wrong people.

This story will be short and deep. When you read my life story remember, "Except for the grace of God, there go I." My life could be yours. If so, I hope you will see how you, too, can change it.

This book filled with information that I pray will lead you to a new chapter in your book called Life.

My parents owned the house where my sisters and I shared a room. The boys had the third floor. The first floor of the two-family home available for rent until we started growing and we all needed more space. As they grew older, my sisters and brothers had they own lives. Everyone acted as if we did not know each other. I was not sure where I fit in. It was like everyone had a plan and I had nothing. Where did I belong? Most days I felt as if I was standing outside looking in the window of a stranger's home. I would say to me, "How could a mother make a difference in her children?" We all had some kind of bond. We knew we were a family; however, I do not think we understood it.

Locked in a Box

The big secret in life is that there is no big secret. Whatever your goal, you can get there if you're willing to work.
Oprah Winfrey

RENÉE JONES

I was born in 1959, in Cleveland, Ohio. I always felt I did not have a place in my family. My mom treated me as if I did not belong. One day while I was still very young, she told me that when I was born she gave me to my older sister to care for as if I were her baby doll. However, I was a person, not a toy.

My oldest sister understood what I was feeling. We all in the family called her SISTER. Therefore, when I talk about her I am going to call her SISTER, as I do today. I remember hearing SISTER say, "That's my baby," talking about me. However, I wanted my mother to say, "That's my baby." I needed my mother's hugs.

My sister under me was the prince in my eyes. Whenever she asked for something, she got it. Whenever I asked, it was different. I am not so sure how, but it was. The way I looked at myself, being a part of the family, there was something wrong. I just did not know what.

When my mother told me she gave me to my sister, it hurt. It hurts when your mother tells you something like that and I really believed her. I waited for her to say whom she gave my younger sisters to, but she never did. I guessed my sisters did not need given away. Whatever I did or whenever I was hurt, my sister came running to me to make it all better. My mother did not show me love. She would make comments that hurt.

Let me ask you something. Do you have some kind of pain in your soul? A hurt that you cannot explain by someone and you are not sure what started that hurt; you just know it is there? Well, that is the feeling I had.

I always wondered why she gave me to my sister. The word "gave" made me think of something thrown away, and that is how it felt to me.

I remember my mother taking my sisters in her arms and telling them she

Locked in a Box

loved them, but I cannot recall her ever holding me like that. What I do remember is mean looks; the kind of looks that said, "Don't you say a word," looks that kept me quiet inside and afraid to come out. In addition, there were hard words; words like, "You're dumb," "You're stupid," "You're just like your father's sister; acting like them people," and many others I have blocked out of my mind.

When I was about eight or nine my mother bought me a pair of eye glasses. I have very bad vision. The right eye is partly blind. Well, I needed those glasses and the lenses were so thick the kids at school teased me, calling me Popeye, Pepsi or Coke Bottle Glasses, all kinds of derogatory names. I came home crying, running to tell my mother, only to hear, "So what? You better wear them." We had to go to the store with our mother and I took the glasses off and hid them in the store. Later that night my mother asked about them. I thought I was going to pass out. However, before I could, she took a cord and minutes later, I had webs on my body, nice long red puffy welts.

One day my stepfather, who I loved dearly, told my mom, "STOP! Leave her alone!" He tried to intervene when she treated my younger sister and me differently. When she would say mean things to me or I could not understand what she wanted me to do.

That day I felt wanted. It felt so good. It was the best day of my childhood to know that my stepdad, Rodney Hill, was there for me. Let me share about my stepdad. My dad would come home every Friday with two gallons of Seagram's Gin, one for the house and one for his car. That was when my mom got mad and ran him out of the house. He would say, "I am having a taste," instead of a drink. However, no matter what, he loved his girls, including me. The funniest times were when he was drunk. He would give us money. Whatever we asked for, he was okay with it. When he did not drink, he would sleep or do yard work. He was the most wonderful person in my life. I loved him so much. Later you will hear how he waited for me to come to him before he moved on to be with God.

The day my mom told me she gave me away, my life changed. I remember she was laughing and drinking. She looked at me and told me, "You belong to your big sister. I gave you to her." That made my feel very uncomfortable. My heart was beating fast. My hands were sweating and my eyes got big. I wanted to turn around and run for my life. I wanted my mother, but I felt alone, different, isolated. My two younger sisters were skinny with long, beautiful hair and light skin. My mom was black and beautiful to me. Everyone in my family was beautiful, but me. I felt ugly and unwanted. To me, whenever I looked in a mirror, I saw a little girl who looked beaten down and scared; a girl with not one drop of beautiful hair, and overweight. In the mirror, I looked lost in my eyes, lonely, and fearful.

Now I understand that my mama did the best she could with me. She did what she felt was right. However, back then you could not tell me my mama loved me.

My mother had her own problems and ghosts in her closet. She had a way of making things happen without my dad. I remember her friends who lived across the street and how they would whisper. I remember the white man who lived in the basement of one of her friends that would always look at my mom in a way that made her smile and dance. I would wonder what it was he had that I did not have to make her happy. I was not sure what was going on, but in my mind, something was going on.

She met the finest man, had good friends, worked every day and cooked all the time. We never ever missed a holiday. I remember her laughing a lot, too. She really enjoyed laughing. One thing, she did not understand when it was time to stop. My mother would drink also, and when she drank, she turned so mean. She would tell us that she could turn into a monster, and she really did.

Though I did not feel my mom wanted me, my sister became the star of my life. I believed she loved me. I like to think we all have someone who is a "star" to us. My sister filled the role of mother for me. I loved my big sister, but I wanted to love my mother and wanted her to love me. I lit up every time I saw my sister, then I would burn out when I saw my mother. My sister would tell me, "I love you more than anyone." The first time I heard that it was from sister.

Sister was twelve years older than I was. One day she sat me down and we were talking about us. She told me how from the time I was little; she would dress me up and hold me all the time. Then she started crying. She told me about a time once when she was outside riding her bike with one of my brothers. She had me with her. I was about six months old at the time. When she took me on that bike ride, my little legs were hanging down and swinging. Suddenly, my foot caught in the wheel, cut the skin off the back of my foot. She felt so much pain about it that she never rode a bike again. I have never seen her ride a bike.

Growing up, I felt I was two people. Hey, I am a Gemini. I was afraid of my mom. When I look back, I can see that I would act or become someone else in order to stop the pain.

One time my mom was cleaning the house. We all had to clean. "Never leave the kitchen or bathroom dirty," she would say. One day I was helping her wash clothes and she sent me down to the basement.

I remember her calling me. I got up and ran to see want she wanted. She said to go to the basement and get the clothes. I just stood there.

"What's wrong?" she said.

I told her, "I can't go down there by myself to get the clothes and bring them outside." I was so scared to go down there.

When I took too long, my mother screamed at me. At that time, I remember, I turned into someone else. It was as if I turned into another person. I was not there for about five minutes. That is how I learned not to feel pain. I placed myself in a box.

You can only understand the meaning of the box if you have been in it. It is hard to get out, but we can recover. Okay, let us move on.

My sister raised me. She tried so hard to give me the best of everything meaning pretty clothes, keeping my hair done, telling me, "Pretty girls don't do that." However, when my sister grew up, she found her own life and left me all alone. Who would help me now? Who would be there to hold me?

I remember one day when my sister came to visit us. My mom wanted her to stay but she would not. Mom tried to hold her back so she would not leave the house. They fought and my sister finally left. With tears running down my face, I watched out my bedroom window as she ran away. That was the day I felt abandoned, not understanding. I had no one to talk to and I have carried that feeling until this day. When a person who was in my life leaves, I feel locked in that box all over again.

I locked myself in the box to cover my feelings. In order to unlock the box, I had to see some things and experience life. Now I look back on my life wondering what I could have done differently. Look at yourself. Have you ever asked the question, "Why me?" or said, "If only...?"I have heard people say all we can do is live the best we can. If that is true, why did it seem my best was never enough?

I know one thing for sure. God has our lives all planned out. I am not sure why all those things happened in my family. All I know is that is what my family has told me and I still feel the pain today. I share my life with you hoping to help you and hoping that you in turn will share yours with someone who needs help.

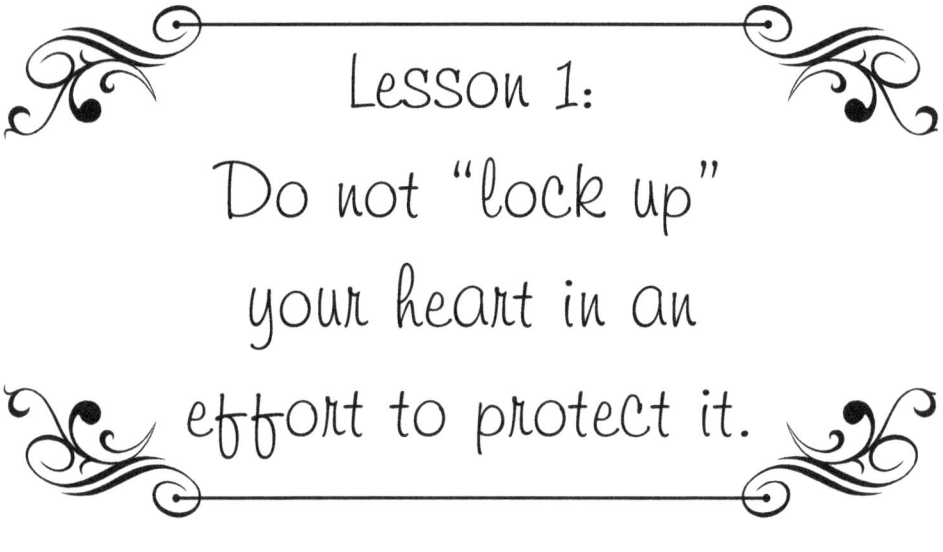

Lesson 1: Do not "lock up" your heart in an effort to protect it.

A Lap Today, a Slap Tomorrow

The secret to a rich life is to have more beginnings than endings.
Dave Weinbaum

I lived in a dark place for years. I wanted to scream, "Why can't they hear me or see me hurt? Why is my mom just walking by me? I am trying to tell her I need her help, but I can't. Please hug me. Please show me the way."

My two little sisters and I received most everything we asked for, but I was still missing something. We moved to East 110th Street off Union in Cleveland, Ohio. At that time, we were the only blacks on the street.

Our best friends lived next door. We played with them every day and night. Then one day they moved away and another black family moved on the street. I could not understand that. I missed my white friends. My brother told my mother to buy us some black dolls to play with.

Our family had parties most every weekend; rent parties, fish fry parties, or "just-because" parties. I was so young I would peek around the corner at people dancing and drinking. I would laugh about it with my sister. Then one time my mother caught me and said, "You better get in that bed!" Oh my goodness, she scared me so much.

My younger sister was very pretty. She was the star in my mother's eyes. My mother made me go everywhere with her so I could be there to protect her. When she got into fights, I ended up fighting her battles. I did not want to fight or to take her places, but if I didn't my mom would get me. In addition, I was not taking any chances with my mom. If my sister got hurt, I got hurt.

For years I asked myself, "Who is going to protect me?" Then one day I said, "I will find someone to protect me," and I began looking for love in all the wrong places.

At one of my mother's parties, a family friend asked me to sit on his lap. I did and when I got down, he gave me fifty cents. Back then, that was a lot of money. All the other kids received ten cents. However, I felt so funny. I didn't care so much about the amount but that was the first time I looked to a man to give me money.

In my family, "What goes on here stays here," so I could not tell anyone. I was afaid my mom would be angry with me for it; not because of herself, but because I was not watching her girls better. I was already in a box. If I had told my mom, the box locked and the lights would go out.

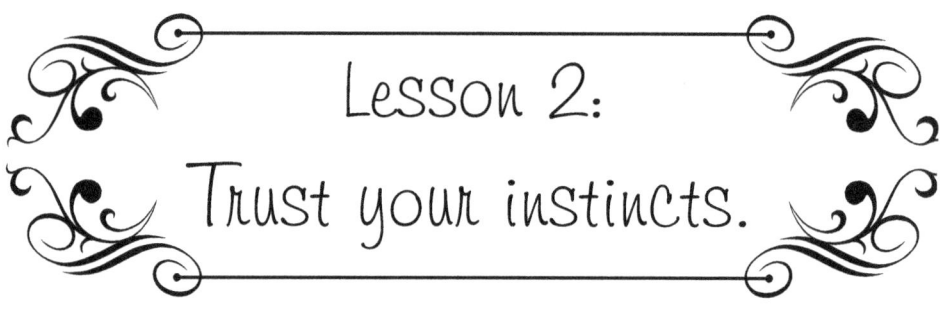

Lesson 2: Trust your instincts.

The Protector

Life's battles don't always go to the stronger or faster man.
But sooner or later the man who wins,
is the man who thinks he can.
Vince Lombardi

When I was still at an early age, my brother came home from the war. I was later told he gave me scarlet fever. The whole house was in danger. I had to live in a room all alone for weeks. The fever left me in a mindset that I was not important to anyone. My sisters and brothers and even the people on our street looked at me as if I were a walking monster.

If I had known God then I would have known that he saved my life. I did not know him then, but I know him now and so do you.

Years went by. It was time for school. Those years I could not deal with life. I was not very smart in class and seemed as if I failed at everything.

Once I came home so happy about the idea of joining the drill team at my middle school. I went to two tryouts. I loved the drill team. I had finally found something I enjoyed. However, I was never able to go back. My mother was not happy about me doing it, so I had to stop.

I spent my school years protecting my little sister. She was the queen at our school. Most everyone loved her. She made the yearbook every year—best dressed, most likely to succeed—best this, best that. Some other girls hated her because they were jealous. She was beautiful, but very mouthy. Often times she was in trouble and fought a lot. I never had a fight of my own, but I had to be the one fighting her battles.

One day she got into it with some girls and that afternoon they jumped her. I knew this was going to happen. Someone told me there was going to be a fight

> *Things we addicts deal with before we take our first hit of anything—a drink or crack—it doesn't matter. A drug is a drug. We have a deeper need that no one can ever understand.*

The Protector

after school. However, I did not want to be there. It was always about her.

When I got home, my brother had a fit. He kept saying, "Where were you?" He told me I had better kick their butts by the time my mom came home from work. We were both in big trouble because I did not do anything about it.

From that day on, I was as a fighter. Everywhere I went or my sister went I had to fight. Now I was not just dealing with loneliness and abandonment. I had to deal with bullying. That was the only way to protect my sister. However, did I like it? NO!

Lesson 3:
It is fine to support and love someone, but remember you have to love yourself first.

Who Could I Talk to Now

How do people make it through life without a sister?
Sara Corpening

More years passed. I was close to one of my brothers then. David was his name. I was able to talk to him like no one else. Then early one morning David's dog went crazy. The phone rang. Someone answered it. I heard a scream. A cry for God was next. It was my mom. That was the day I lost David, a boy who never had a fight, who was very quiet and sweet. He was suddenly gone. It felt as if God had taken him from me.

Now whom could I talk to? Who would listen? Eight months pregnant with my second child, I ran down the street looking for the person who did this. I could not find anyone to blame.

I was in an abusive marriage when my brother died. My husband and I married because my mom and his dad said to marry. We did not know each other.

We had sex the first time then one month later, I was with child. For him, I was not the only one. Why is it so easy for one and not the other?

Before long, I found myself with two boys and a husband. I could not cook. I did not know how to treat a husband or take care of kids. All I knew was how to clean. I worked and he slept. While I was working, the boys stayed with their dad's mom. It was 1979. He got a good job at Ford Motor Company and in 1982, fired because he would never go to work. He stayed home to watch me.

I had to ride the bus to work because he kept the only car we had. It took fifteen minutes to walk home from the bus stop. One day I arrived home, hungry and tired. I turned the key in the door and opened it. An hour later, I woke up on the floor. My husband told me to get up and cook dinner.

Never hit before. I had always won all my fights. I did not understand why he had hit me and I was afraid to ask WHY. I could not look at myself.

If your mate has ever hit you once, you have heard this: "Oh, baby, I didn't mean it. Please forgive me. It is stress. It will never happen again."

Then you say, "It is okay."

Once he hears this, he knows you are in his hands. It is not okay!

Then the lovemaking comes. It may seem like the best you have ever had.

As you know if this has happened to you, that first hit turned into beatings repeatedly. It had been three years of, "I'm sorry, please forgive me. I'll never do it again."

Lesson 4: God loves you. Each morning we wake up, we have a fresh start! Talk with God.

Please Stop the Pain

The golden moments in the stream of life rush past us and we see nothing but sand; the angels come to visit us, and we only know them when they are gone.
George Elliot

It was the night before my birthday. My sons and I had been home alone having fun all day. My husband came home from work or somewhere about 9pm. I do not remember what really started it, but I am sure it was something like, "The dinner is cold. Why did you walk away from me? What did you say to me?"

> *You think you need that man that's beating you? Before you let that good job he has get in the way of the truth, sit down and write yourself a letter.*
>
> ASK YOURSELF THIS: *Do I really love him or her? Do I really understand love?*

I was in the bedroom putting the boys, ages two and four, to bed. He grabbed my neck. The last thing I remember was looking at the fear in my boys' faces. The next day I found myself on the floor where he had left me not knowing if I was dead or alive.

I could not move one side of my body and I could not see. "Dear God, what's going on? Please help me and help me now," I prayed.

I could hear my sons playing. I heard my oldest say, "Where is my mommy?"

It was my birthday, May 24, 1981, when my husband beat me to the point I had two black eyes, a busted lip, a broken jaw and other injuries.

The day after that, bruised and broken, he sent me to the store. I took the money he gave me to buy his cigarettes and got on the #15 bus. People were looking and whispering. They could see me badly beaten, but no one helped me. I rode the bus downtown. I did not care who saw me, what they thought or what they said. I needed out and I was ready.

I walked into the police station in downtown Cleveland, Ohio. For the first time in my life, I felt the protection I had always wanted from the officers who arrested my husband.

> ### PLEASE STOP THE PAIN
> *If you are in a love triangle and you think he loves you, right now you feel there's no hope. You think no one cares and it's too late for you. Please know you are not alone. I am here with you along with countless others. Set a plan. Make the call now.*
>
> ### NATIONAL HOT LINE FOR DOMESTIC VIOLENCE (DV)
> ### 1-800-799-7233
> ### JUST SAY HELLO

The four officers who sat at the front desk all came to my rescue. They took me in and walked me through the process of recovery. One took me to the back. Another did a report. The other two talked about going to get my husband. I also met a woman. She turned into my savior. She walked me to the end of the hall, opened the door and went in with me to the Domestic Violence Center.

After the police took pictures of my face and body, the emergency team came and took me to the closet Emergency Room (ER) where I was treated. I had the nurse call my sister. Oh, but my family always came and tried to save the day. My sister beat the "you-know-what" out of him for hitting me. She got my sons and came to the ER.

The police brought him in. He was fighting them. Now, if that is not crazy! He thinks he can beat me AND the police! He went to jail, but of course, his dad got him out.

After a day or two in the hospital I had to go back home. My sons were there when I returned with my support from Domestic Violence. The fear was gone. All I had on my mind was my pain. I thought if I have to die in the name of love, then I am not in love.

In my marriage, it was July or August 1978 when the beatings started. For three years, I had endured black eyes, a bleeding mouth, and many more injuries in places you could not see. The time had come to make my move. I told myself everything had to come together now. My husband left home to go to work. I called my mother. She had my brothers come get me. We packed, and within three hours, we had moved everything into a two-bedroom apartment.

> **The Great Escape**
>
> **Plan 1:** Save money; every dollar, every penny.
> **Plan 2:** Find a place to go.
> **Plan 3:** Start packing a little each day, things he will not miss.
> **Plan 4:** Don't give up. Keep on moving. Tell yourself, "I can do this.
> **Plan 5:** DO NOT TURN AROUND.
>   I am strong."
> *If the abuse is too bad, there are shelters and money is no issue.*

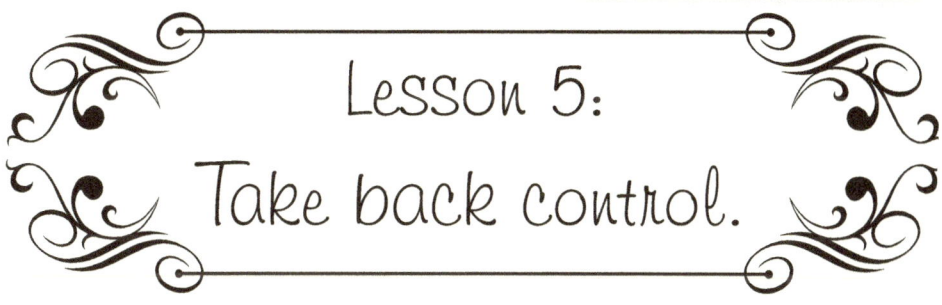

Lesson 5: Take back control.

I can be changed by what happens to me, but I refuse to be reduced by it.
Maya Angelou

In the Name of Love

No legacy is so rich as honesty.
William Shakespeare

Can you imagine my night once he opened the door to that apartment? He came to my mother's home looking for me, threatening everyone. My mother called the police. This was the last time the police charged him. He did a very short amount of time in jail. While he was there, I was downtown filing for divorce. We went to court and the judge ordered him to pay $25 per week for each of our kids. I walked away a happy woman, but still with fear of what he might do.

He went on with his life. I was free. However, I was lost. I did not know what to do or how to do it. My mother did not understand. I prayed for guidance. I had not finished school. I had two sons and no money. However, I was not going back. I knew I could do this. The fight was over. It was up to me to find the support I needed.

We moved in with my mother. I got a job. The boys' grandmother on their father's side kept them more than I did, which at that time, I felt was a good thing. Once I moved into my own apartment near the family, I felt better about myself and had hope.

Let me tell you, it might seem like the pain will not stop, never go away. However, it will. I am here today only because I loved me and my sons more then I loved that man. It is a great feeling when you break loose, when you take off the chains.

It does not take long to start going out looking for love, something I never had and never understood. I remember going to a club every week for months, standing against the wall. One night I noticed a man watching me. Our eyes locked. He walked over to me. I felt something in my soul. He smelled so good. He was tall and had a smooth way about him. We exchanged numbers. After we talked all night, he took me to breakfast, held my hand and walked me to the door before he left. I just knew he was the

In the Name of Love

one I had been looking for.

The next day he called. We went out and spent the whole day together. I had never ridden in a Mercedes Benz before. I felt important. He told me he could fall in love with me. That was the last word in love. For me, it did not take long.

About two weeks later, he took me downtown for a ride. He showed me the prostitutes on the streets walking around in heels and see-through clothing. That morning we went shopping for heels and fishnet stockings. He had me put them on and gave me some condoms. We rode around looking for a street corner for me. When he found the right one, he popped the door locks and told me to get out. There I stood, alone.

A man pulled up and asked me to come to the car. I got in. After that trick, I saw I could make some money. It became fun. I enjoyed the streets, the competition between me and the other women. The other pimps wanted me. WOW! I felt like a star. Pimps were trying to buy me. Their hookers wanted me in their stables. I was so clueless to the real deal, all in the name of love.

This went on for months. I did not think the women of the night would tell on me. For a while, I was the only girl that vice did not mess with. I watched the police ride by with cars full of hookers and I kept on with my business. I was not expecting a trap. I had a different look about me. I just knew I was better than the others were.

I did not know the others were telling vice I was one of them. One Saturday morning vice laid back in the cut and watched. The very first trick, vice was there and asked me to get into the car.

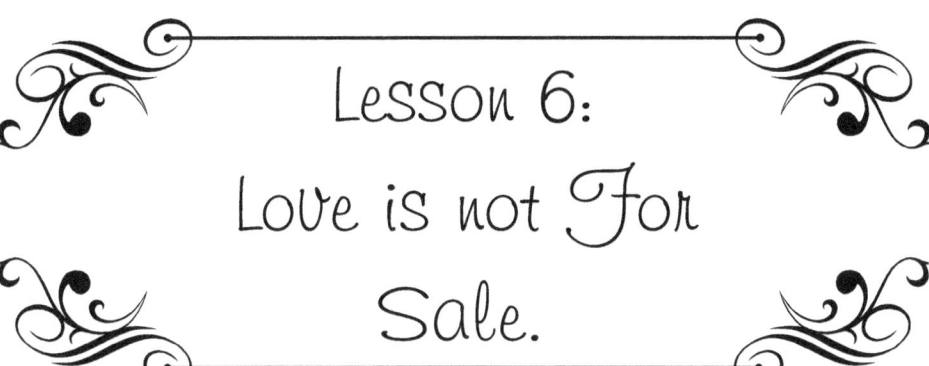

Lesson 6: Love is not For Sale.

If I had permitted my failures, or what seemed to me at the time a lack of success, to discourage me I cannot see any way in which I would ever have made progress.
Calvin Coolidge

The Key to My Jail

All God's angels come to us disguised.
James Russell Lowell

Jail was new to me. Back then, if arrested during the weekend you stayed in jail until Monday. At first, it was fun. I saw myself in and out of the system. Judges knew me by name. There was one judge, who turned into my savior. When we first met, she asked me, "Why are you here?" She asked me to meet her in her chambers. I did. In addition, from that day in 1984 until now, she has done outstanding things for me and said wonderful words like, "I believe in you." One day in court she said, "You are not listening. When are you going to stop, Ms. Jones? I will help you."

She sent me to jail. Her last words were, "Your man has the key to the jail." I did not understand that for a long time. Finally, I realized that if I would stop and leave him, I would be free.

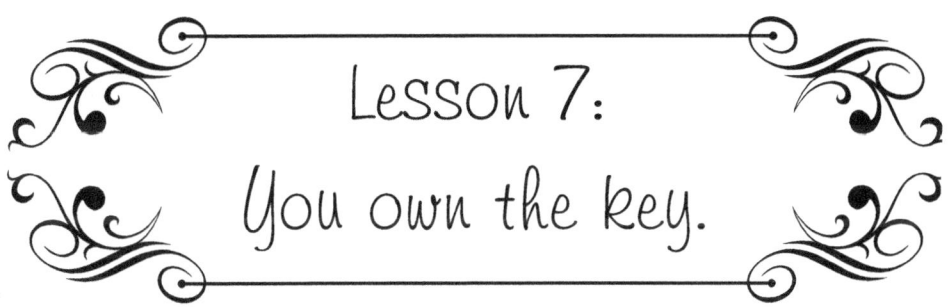

Lesson 7: You own the key.

Love all, trust a few, do wrong to none.
William Shakespeare

Freedom Isn't Free

Once you choose hope, anything's possible.
Christopher Reeve

After six months, I got out of the workhouse. However, I returned to the streets. Keep in mind that all of this was a search for love. I remember one day I was tired and wanted to stop. I called my mother and asked her if I could come home. She told me yes. However, when I got there, within an hour, I heard her talking to her husband (at the time). She came into the room where I was and asked me to give her all the money I had. I would make all the money the night before. Then she told me I could not stay there. She wanted to go to bed. She had to lock her house and I had to leave.

I had nowhere to go. I realized the streets were the only place for me. Can you imagine how I felt? My heart crushed. I felt like that little girl again that she did not care for. I looked at my mother and said to myself, "WHY ME?" Today I understand. I lived and fought through this to carry this message of hope to you. For a reason only God knows, he wanted me to feel the pain to save you.

Sometime later, I ended up back in the place I was running from. I wondered, "How do I get out of this?" When the streets started getting hard and making money was slow, I called my sister once again. A man once told me, "Freedom isn't free." However, I wanted freedom.

I want to be free. Here is how I did it. When I left, I meant to stay stopped. No more trick or treats. It was time for the real world. I had to grow up. When I made up my mind, I got a house and a job. I worked in a bar on Kinsman Avenue in Cleveland, Ohio. I started as a cocktail server. I had several men smiling, tipping and bringing gifts. When the owners gave me a key and placed me behind the bar, my thinking told me, "Girl, you got it going on."

Then it happened.

Lesson 8: Do not sell yourself short.

A Sandwich Bag

*God will not look you over for medals,
degrees or diplomas, but for scars.*
Elbert Hubbard

A family member gave me a sandwich bag of powder to sell behind the bar. The money was coming in for the bar and for me. I wanted a better way to live. The best part about working in a bar was the afternoon. At that time, I was not using drugs or drinking. I was making money fast and honestly.

> Often alcohol- or drug-impaired persons have no idea how obvious their difficulties are to so many other people. When they are finally confronted, it can be a great shock to find out how much of their behavior that they thought was hidden was, in fact, observed. The rationalization and denial systems actually convince the alcohol-impaired person that no one on the job or in the community knows about a drinking problem.
>
> From the book LOOSENING THE GRIP
> By Jean Kinney

This went on about two years, selling powder under the counter, in the bathroom or outside. Everybody wanted to be my friend. I remembered the beginning of my life. All I ever wanted was for someone to love me and hang out with me. I finally felt like I belonged. I enjoyed the feeling of want and need for the first time in my life. I not only belonged, I was in demand.

I met a female in the bar one night. At closing, she would not go home. She kept saying, "I am going with you and your friends." At first, I thought she was the police. It was time to lock the doors. She just would not leave. When I moved, she moved. I had no idea who she was and I just wanted to take a man home and sell some dope. She said she did not have a car so I told her, "Come on. You can go with me."

A Sandwich Bag

Therefore, this stranger got in the car with me. We talked and she seemed to be cool. When we arrived at my house, we all sat around. She asked me for some dope. She paid for the first hit. The second one, she asked for credit. There were drugs all over the table, my partner has and mine.

This went on for weeks. One night she asked me to come into the kitchen. My friends warned me not to fall prey to her, but I was naïve and vulnerable.

Well, I went in the kitchen. She was cooking. I asked, "What are you doing?"

"Wait till I'm done," she said. "I want you to try something."

On that day, I turned my life over to crack cocaine. My heart breaks over the people I harmed when I was addicted to crack. That day I had a sandwich bag of dope. Within a short few hours, it was gone. I was alone in the house with my new so-called friend whom I did not know. Everyone else left after my first hit.

Being a crack-head is hard work. We are always searching for more. **A life we think we are in control of**. The crack game took me to a place I did not get out of for years. I had to get more drugs. Everything in the house went. Other people went. I stole and sold to get more. If a dope dealer asked me to do something, I did it for one more hit.

As a crack-head, I found other crack-heads. I moved from the east side of town to the west side. A very close family friend helped me get in a housing program where I would own the house in one year. I passed all the requirements to get into the program. The monthly rent was only $125.00. I did well for the first two months. After that, I could not pay the rent. I was working, making good money. However, after a month, I quit. Now it was food stamps and government checks. I thought I could handle the high, but the high handled me.

I went up and down the streets all night, leaving my sons in the house, to look for a hit. My sister fed up. She came over the day, walked in the house, left the door open and told me I was moving to Alabama. I screamed at her, "I'm not a crack-head. I am doing fine. Leave me the fuck alone!"

Lesson 9: Carry your own baggage and let everyone else carry their baggage.

*We should not look back unless it is to derive useful lessons
from past errors, and for the purpose of profiting
by dearly bought experience.*
George Washington

Left to Find a Husband

Character is higher than intellect.
Ralph Waldo Emerson

My boys and I moved to Birmingham, Alabama. I am not sure why my sister talked me into leaving Cleveland, but I do know what she said in order for me to leave my dope-head friends and free babysitters. She had to tell me something good, and she did. My sister told me if I would move to Alabama I would find a husband. So we moved. She paid the rent for a year so we would have a safe place to stay.

Once I got there, I watched the people around the apartments. I searched for those just like me. What I found was a drug dealer. Hey, even better, I thought. In the apartment

> I am so grateful today that she did not give up on me. She told me if I moved I would find a husband. You should know I still don't have one.

with my sons, I watched this person for about fifteen minutes. It seemed like hours. I had to get his attention! I took out the trash. I knew he was watching me. I could not understand why he did not say anything to me.

I had to try one more time. I took some newspapers and put them in a trash bag. I walked to the dumpster again, this time more slowly. Finally, he called, "Hey, what's up?"

I turned around. "Are you talking to me?"

"Ya!" he responded. "What are you doing over there?" The voice was strong, the face was smooth, but the spirit was not there.

Here I go, I thought. However, I told myself, "I ain't doin' nothing." As I walked around in the apartment, I opened the patio door so he could see me. I was trying to let him know I was there all alone. He walked over and spoke to me over the bushes then moved closer. I invited him in.

Left to Find a Husband

My disease started to take over. I rubbed on him, kissed his ear, and I distracted him until he forgot what he had in his pocket. With one of my hands on that special part of his body, I slipped the other in that special pocket, the one where he kept the dope. Once I had it in my hand, all bets were off. Then the other part of me came out. I asked him to leave. I did not have all the tools I needed to get high, but one thing for sure, an addict will find tools to work with and I did. The race began. My addiction kicked in and kicked in fast and hard. With my sons sleeping away in their beds, that night I smoked all I had stolen.

Then I heard a window crash. A few minutes later, someone was banging on the front door. I opened it to find that same man, the drug dealer, with a gun. He pushed me into the living room. He stood in the same spot he had been when he was last in my apartment. He placed the gun to my head and told me if he did not get his dope back, he was going to kill me. My disease had me crazy. I somehow convinced him that I did not have it and he finally left.

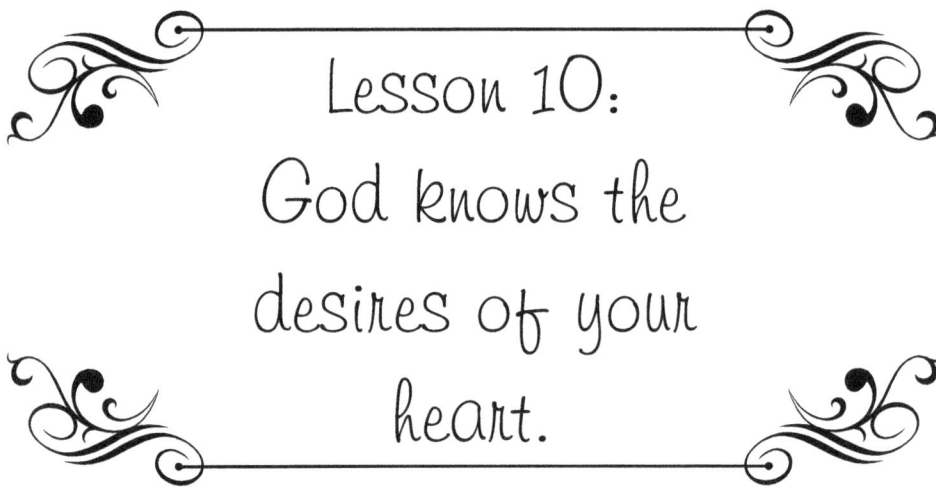

Lesson 10: God knows the desires of your heart.

Twenty Dollar High

*Before you pray, forgive. Before you quit, try.
Before you retire, save. Before you die, give.*
William Arthur Ward

It is easy for an active user to find another. I walked up the street in that new city and there they all stood. Therefore, I made myself the best friend to strangers. I had ten dollars. Someone else had three. We all worked up twenty dollars to get high—a twenty for three addicts.

As time went on, I tried to fill the role of a good mother. I walked my sons to school. I went to the P.T.O. meetings and school events. I have to know the teachers. This went on for about six months. Then the dope would not let me walk my sons to school anymore. My life was just about getting high.

WOW! This went repeatedly. The lease was up and it was time to move. I received a call from my sister telling me my dad was very sick. My stepfather, Rodney Hill, God rest his soul, was an alcoholic for as many years as I could remember. He had a good job, but every Friday he would buy two gallons of Seagram's Gin, one for the house and one for his car. That was the reason for the fights my mom and dad would have every weekend. He had so many things wrong with him. I felt bad that crack would not let me see about the only man who really loved me, who protected me and would tell me how special I was. I wanted to come, Daddy. I missed you then and I miss you now.

He knew I was a crack-head. He just did not know if I was all right. I am not sure why I had to go to Cleveland, Ohio, but I went. My sister kept asking me if I was going to go see Daddy. I was afraid of what I might see so for a while I did not go. The next day I knew I had to go see him. My heart kept telling me this was it. I went with my sister. As I slowly walked into the room, the feeling I would had the night before kept showing up. The closer I got to his bed, the stronger the feeling got. The nurse came in to check a machine. When she left I moved closer. I leaned down to him and said, "Daddy, I am just fine. I promise you I will get better. I love you."

Twenty Dollar High

That man could not and had not moved in over two years. That day, after I stepped back, his eyes moved along with one of his fingers.

I went back to Alabama. Two days later, I got a phone call. My dad had died. I felt good because I knew he had been waiting for me to come before he let go. Thank you, God, for that time with my dad.

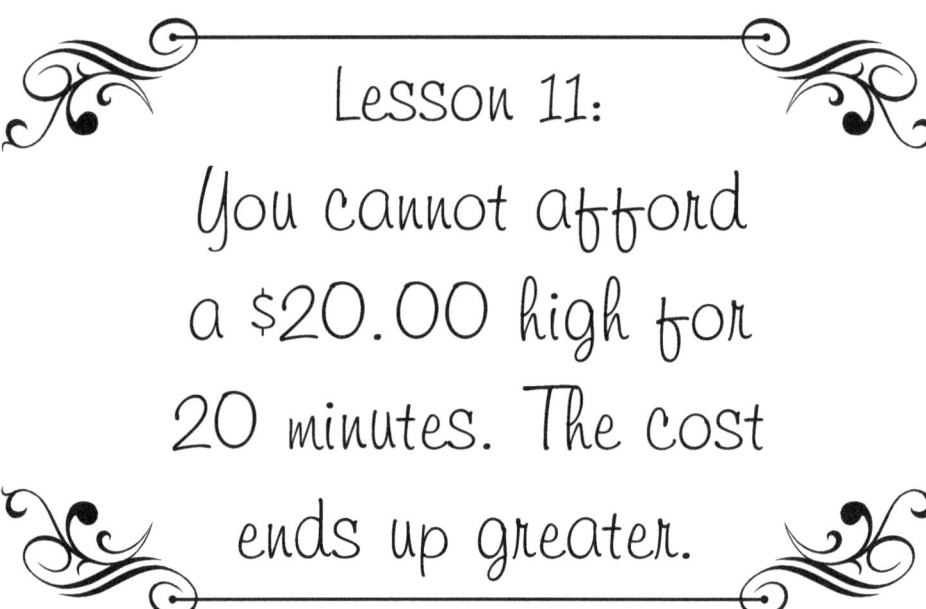

Lesson 11: You cannot afford a $20.00 high for 20 minutes. The cost ends up greater.

I Took Me with Me

*The existence of forgetting has never been proved:
We only know that some things don't come to mind
when we want them.*
Friedrich Nietzsche

Once again, I went back to the streets. I was trying not to, but the drugs were calling me back. The dope told me, "I'm your daddy now." My life was empty without my dad and overfull with my mother, if you know what I mean.

> *The best and most beautiful things in the world cannot be seen or even touched. They must be felt with the heart.*
> By Helen Keller

For LOVE, all I found was a "PIMP" man. He wined and dined me for three days. The fourth date he said, "I would like you to do something for me. Let's take a ride." The late night ride was not looking at the stars. It was looking at the women of the night walking the streets. The next day I was walking with them.

Here I was thinking I was a real good "hoe" only to find out today that in 2008 we all were real good "hoes." However, one thing for sure: MAMA AIN'T TEACH ME THAT! Do not worry, my sister did not teach me that either.

Well, that went on for about two years. In addition, it got deeper. You see, my life, the first life, was all about looking for LOVE. We did not say "I LOVE YOU" in the home I grew up in, but I knew it was out there. I looked for love in the tricks, the abuser, and the family. I clicked my heels three times repeatedly and over again thinking I would be some place, only to open my eyes in the same place.

I stayed in New Orleans for about one year then moved back home to Cleveland, Ohio. One thing I learned: Wherever I went, I took me with me. Now here I was with the disease of addiction and my job title was smoking crack. I had twenty-two years of experience doing anything and everything

I Took Me with Me

to get one more. You name it; I am sure I have done it.

I have come across some good men. You probably know some among your friends and family. They told me, the way to a man's heart is through his stomach. Well, MAMA AIN'T TEACH ME THAT. However, before God could bless me with anyone, I had to clean myself up.

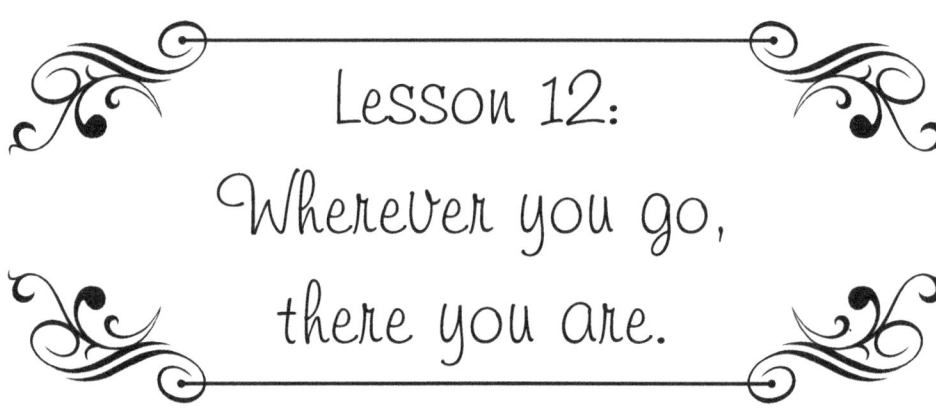

Lesson 12: Wherever you go, there you are.

The Start of the New Life

Memory... *is the diary that we all carry about with us.*
Oscar Wilde

I look back and remember I never gave up on God. I knew he would save me from the car I jumped out of, the items I stole, the man that robbed me with a gun in my face, and the rapist.

I tried to stop the drugs, but I could not. I needed more and more. A friend of mine at that time called me to come over. She said a person was there with some good dope, I did not think to take a good look at him, but he took a good look at me. After two years, he remembered that I had taken his dope out of his pocket.

I had my last twenty at the house and I had a great idea—high as I could be—with a great idea. I asked for his number. Within two hours, I went home and made the call. He came right over. He was outside waiting for me. I spent the twenty on the first rock. The second, he gave me. For the third, he placed a rock on the stem.

Nothing is like the very first hit. If you are looking for the very first hit again, you will never, never get it. You are now a trick for the crack. I spaced out. I ran to the bathroom. Once I came out, he was standing there. He grabbed my neck and pulled me into the bedroom. He beat me repeatedly and raped me repeatedly with my boys in the next room. I knew if I screamed or resisted he could kill us all. All I could do was say, "Please, no." Silently, I begged God to make it stop. Today I understand that NO means NO. He had no right to beat and rape me.

I remember my middle child the next day looking at me.

{ *National Sexual Assault Hotline 1-800-656-HOPE*

Call. Someone is there waiting. Just say, "Hello." }

The Start of the New Life

Lesson 13: Thank God for second chances.

She Was Not Joking

You get what you think about, whether you want it or not.
Commit to thinking about what you want, rather than
how impossible or difficult that dream may seem.
Dr. Wayne W. Dyer, *Being in Balance*

In February 2000, I had about $2,000 dollars. I was getting high every day, all day, until one day something went wrong. I looked in the mirror. I could not see the big beautiful brown eyes, the baby doll smile. I could see through myself. My soul was gone. My spirit was gone.

I stood there for a very long time. My sons were calling me. "Mom, are you okay? What are you doing, Mom?"

Then God came to me in the mirror. I began to cry. The only thing I could say to him was, "IF YOU HELP ME, I PROMISE I'LL HELP THOSE JUST LIKE ME." Then God left.

With $247.00 left, I went into treatment. For about four days, everything went good. Then my counselor told me I would never make it. I did not understand why she would say that to me.

I had always had a mindset that I was different from other women. On the seventh day, called into the office, I thought they were going to give me an award or something. However, what happened was not fair. My counselor and two other women were in the room. The Director asked me, "Do you have this guy's bracelet? Are you passing notes to him?"

Unknowingly, not allowed to talk to the men, I had to pack my clothes and go. She should have told me. I thought she was joking. I was waiting for the punch line. However, she was not joking.

All I could do was cry. "I felt so lonely. Please, please, don't put me out," I said to the Director.

"You should have thought of that before you broke the rules," she said. No one told me not to talk to the men. They would say, "Ladies, get numbers when the outside group comes in." Therefore, I did.

Later that night, I left. My baby sister picked me up. I cannot begin to tell you how I felt. I cannot describe the look my sister gave me. I wanted to stop using drugs. I went home and stayed in my room for two days thinking that my sons must be so mad at me. How could I be so dumb?

Man, I wanted to stop using. For the first time in my life, the treatment center gave me hope.

I left the treatment center on February 14 and I have been clean from that day until now.

PROMISES TO GOD

Ask yourself, "How will I or have I kept my promise to God?" List your promises and sign your name.

_____
_____
_____
_____
_____
_____
_____
_____

The courage to change the things I can,
_____

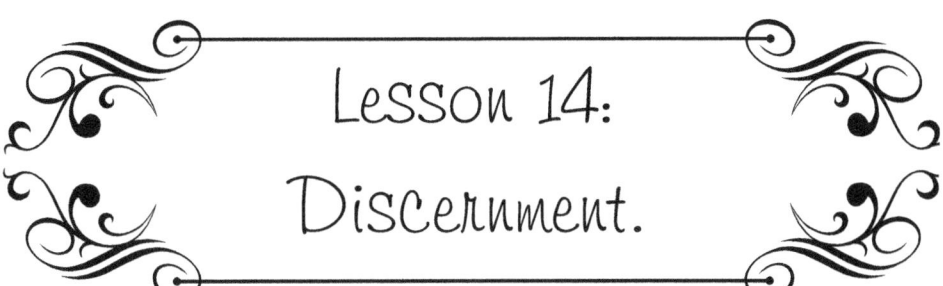

Lesson 14: Discernment.

You don't have to be great to start, but you have to start to be great.
Joe Sabah

You Will Find Haters

Seven days without prayer makes one weak.
Allen E. Vartlett

Renée Jones

I was going through some hard times. I had a good job working for a top retail store. I was going to meetings and enjoying my sons, but my insides were not right. Something was missing. Therefore, I took a drive and got lost in the old neighborhood. Crying and praising God, I found myself in front of an empty house. I parked. Yes, I was tripping out, but I went into the house.

A man painting the walls said, "This must be for you."

"No, I don't think so," I said. "Do you own this house? Can I look around?"

"It's not my house," he answered, "but sure; you can take your time."

There was no fear. I felt safe being in that empty house with a stranger. I asked God why I was there. About fifteen minutes later, God said, "It's time to keep your promise to me."

I asked for the owner's number. After one week of praying and seeking information, I understood what God wanted from me. The time had come to keep the promise I had made to Him. I had to open transitional housing for the lost women out on the streets. No matter whether they came from prison or the penthouse, they needed me to understand and guide them to a safe place.

I had a 401k at that time. I took out $10,000 to get going. I went to meet with a person that owned a transitional house for males to get information I needed to get started. He was strong in the community. I had watched him use people and carry the power of control. In addition, I wanted that same power.

God moved so fast in my life. All the footwork done, I received all the permits for the house. The word was out and the women came. Then more women came to ask me to help them get started. I would say to them, "What is your motive?" If they wanted to make money, my answer was always the same then and now. "I can't help you make money. I can help you help others."

> *Be careful who you place your soul with. What looks good may not be good for you.*

There was one house. Then God opened another. We had two transitional houses and a waiting list. When you do anything to help others and you step outside yourself, you will find haters. I had some that said they were my friends come over to help. The same people who talked about God and love stole from me or called the Health Department on me.

I felt so much bitterness about that until I stopped and prayed. What I found out was that God was letting me feel the hurt I had given others. No matter if they were dope dealers, I did steal and play the game.

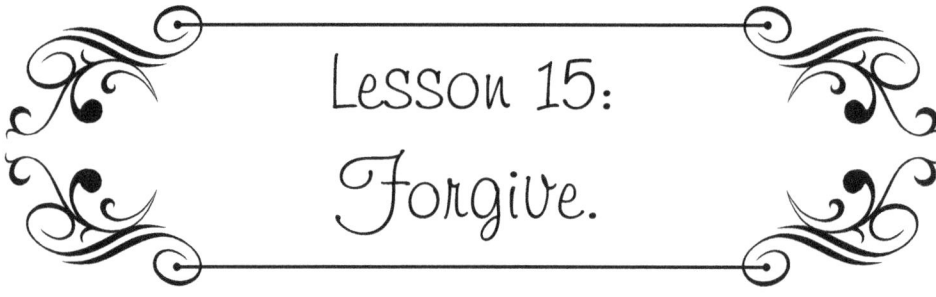

Lesson 15: Forgive.

He Loves Me

The ultimate measure of a man is not where he stands in moments of comfort and convenience, but where he stands at times of challenge and controversy.
Martin Luther King Jr

Then the set-up man, the same one I went to for help on the housing, called me with this bright idea and I fell for it. After one year of paying him $1,700 for rent, he changed. He said things to me and tried to take over the house I had been renting from him. He told me things I could not do, only because I had changed. I was $300.00 short on the rent.

My mind was tight. All I was doing was thinking that if I did this with him I could "use." I had been three years clean. I realized I could not use nor did I want to be used. I stood in my house once again. I locked myself in the same childhood box. Days and weeks went by. I did not eat. The people who said they loved me talked about me. I prayed repeatedly. I called my sister and told her I was going to kill myself. I could see myself driving into a tree. I was ready. That look came back, the same look in the mirror as when I was smoking crack. Only this time I had no drugs in me.

A few more days went by. My sister called to check on me. She talked me into moving back to Cleveland, Ohio, to be with her. I did, but I went untreated for the sickness I had. Depression is deadly. I knew it could take me out. I could not shake it. I went to Cleveland and started working, but I felt crazy.

{ NATIONAL SUICIDE HOTLINE 1-800-273-TALK (8255) }

I made a doctor appointment. He was the best doctor for me. He saved my life. He did not take no for an answer. He kept me in the hospital, and then sent me to a mental health place. Those few days there were the best days of my life. I had nothing to worry about because I was safe. Juanita Bynum said it best: "HE LOVES ME." He loved me. When I was a crack head, a whore, a thief and a disrespectful child, God forgave me and I forgave me.

NARCOTICS ANONYMOUS 1-888-GET-HOPE 1-888-438-4673

Today I am stronger and better. What about you, are you stronger? You may be just like me or you may think we do not understand, but we do. Find a 12-Step meeting.

We are not victims; we are victory.

 Lesson 16:

The first step is the hardest, but do not make it your last step.

Epilogue

Risk more than others think is safe. Care more than others think is wise. Dream more than others think is practical. Expect more than others think is possible.
Cadet Maxim

Today, in 2011, I live in Cleveland, Ohio. I still see my same doctor and work to save lives and give hope to others. My sons are my joy. They are doing wonderfully. My oldest has two beautiful boys who call me every day to check on their "NANA."

My middle boy has forgiven me. He is learning to know his mother. I need to say to you, I am so sorry I hurt you. However, I cannot take away that hurt. You have to do it, but I can pray and ask God to help you and give all of you back to me. I LOVE YOU. If you have to use the numbers, remember I will be there for you as you were there for me.

My baby boy graduated from high school in 2009. He did not let the past of his mom and the system that he was placed in stop him from progressing in life. He is now working and volunteering with youths, has his own apartment and a beautiful girlfriend that supports him. I ask God to give him wisdom for college.

My mother, I write this to tell the world you did the best you could, and the most that we, your children, would let you. In addition, I thank God for our love for each other today.

To the counselor who told me I would never be anything, thank you. I did not "use" no matter what.

For all of you that God has placed in my life, would you give me a chance to show you what God has done for me? Thank you. I am now an author and a nationally- and internationally-known speaker.

In addition, I will always help others. I LOVE YOU ALL.

TELL YOURSELF "I love me" today. Thank you.

Epilogue

Write yourself a letter or write someone else a letter. Then give him or her this book.

Letters from Loved Ones

Life appears to be too short to be spent in nursing animosity or registering wrong.
Charlotte Bronte

Renée,
You made it all the times you said, "I am just fine." It is showing now; you are just fine.

I am not always good with words, but know that I love you. Our mother had four boys before I finally got a sister. I cared for you, I taught you, and when I look back, I think, as you got older you tried to be me. I am so sorry for not being there when you needed me and for the mistakes, I made. However, I did not have A BIG SISTER LIKE YOU DID AND I HELD THAT POSITION WELL.

Congrats and continue helping others,
Sister

Renée,
Told that big girls do not cry, I most often heard from big sisters. Guess what I found out, big girls do cry! Although we do not always cry tears, we cry. You were crying for help many years, but because you were my BIG sister, I did not hear you cry and for that, I would like to say, "I am sorry." You endured so much. Betrayed by friends and misunderstood by family members and yet you prevailed and for that, I applaud you. Today, you have positioned yourself to be there and provide counsel and comfort for those who mirrored your life and you reach out to your nieces and nephews to make sure they are all right, and for that, I would like to say THANK YOU and I LOVE YOU!

Baby Sister,
Lauren

Letters from Loved Ones

To my first aunt Renée,
We grew up together, so I have always felt like you were my big sister. You always made me feel safe and loved.

I do not know when your course took the wrong turn. All I know is that I loved you NO matter what! I am not the type of person who dwells on the past. I just remember once you started coming around, I enjoyed you.

Thank you,
Treasure

Mom,
I remember being homeless after the abuse of my father and hearing you scream when beaten. If there were good times back then, I do not remember anything but the hitting, pain, and living with my grandma as you were trying to get your life back. I remember feeling sick a lot from not seeing you in months. I had to grow up. With no man in the house, I had a lot of responsibility with two younger brothers to look after. When I was eight, I remember when you stepped off the bus and I felt saved from the lack of motherhood. I did not know right away that you were on drugs. I remember being thirteen and my friend's brother sold you crack. My friend told me, but I did not believe him and stopped talking to him. I did not really want to believe it, but with no lights in the house, I had to live with it. Now, Mom, you have been clean eleven years. God is in the middle of things and I am so thankful. Our GOD IS AMAZING!

Love,
KEN D'EL

RENÉE JONES

Letter to Mom

Use this space to write a short letter to your mom, if she did not teach you something, you wish she had.

God, grant me the serenity to accept the things I cannot change.

Sign your name_____

RESOURCES

Alcoholics Anonymous	www.aa.org
Child Abuse Hotline	1-800-422-4453
Cocaine Help Line	1-800-262-2463
Domestic Violence Hotline	1-800-799-7233
Drug/Alcohol Abuse	1-800-662-HELP
Eating Disorders Center	1-888-236-1188
Ecstasy Addiction	1-800-468-6933
Gamblers Anonymous	www.gamblersanonymous.org
Gay & Lesbian National Hotline	1-888-843-4564
Gay & Lesbian Youth/Adults	1-800-850-8078
HIV/AIDS National Hotline	1-800-342-2437
National Dating Abuse Helpline	1-866-331-9474
	www.loveisrespect.org
Overeaters Anonymous	www.oa.org
Rape, Abuse, Incest National Hotline	1-800-656-4673
Runaway Hotline	1-800-621-4000
STD Hotline	1-800-227-8922
Substance Abuse Mental Health Services Administration	
http://www.samhsa.gov	1-877-726-4727
Suicide & Crisis Hotline	1-800-999-9999
Suicide Prevention for Teen Helpline	1-800-400-0900
Teen Suicide Hotline	1-800-621-4000
Victim Center	1-800-394-2255

Books on Treatment Improvement Protocols (TIPs) -
http://www.ncbi.nlm.nih.gov/books/NBK14119/

12 Guiding Principles of Recovery

1. There are many pathways to recovery.
2. Recovery is self-directed and empowering.
3. Recovery involves a personal recognition of the need for change and transformation.
4. Recovery is holistic.
5. Recovery has cultural dimensions.
6. Recovery exists on a continuum of improved health and wellness.
7. Recovery is supported by peers and allies.
8. Recovery emerges from hope and gratitude.
9. Recovery involves a process of healing and self-redefinition.
10. Recovery involves addressing discrimination and transcending shame and stigma.
11. Recovery involves (re)joining and (re)building a life in the community.
12. Recovery is a reality. It can, will, and does happen.

---

1. There are many pathways to recovery. Individuals are unique with specific needs, strengths, goals, health attitudes, behaviors and expectations for recovery. Pathways to recovery are highly personal, and generally involve a redefinition of identity in the face of crisis or a process of progressive change. Furthermore, pathways are often social, grounded in cultural beliefs or traditions and involve informal community resources, which provide support for sobriety. The pathway to recovery may include one or more episodes of psychosocial and/or pharmacological treatment. For some, recovery involves neither treatment nor involvement with mutual aid groups. Recovery is a process of change that permits an individual to make healthy choices and improve the quality of his or her life.

2. Recovery is self-directed and empowering. While the pathway to recovery may involve one or more periods of time when activities are directed or guided to a substantial degree by others, recovery is fundamentally a self-directed process. The person in recovery is the "agent of recovery" and has the authority to exercise choices and make decisions based on his or her recovery goals that have an impact on the process. The process of recovery leads individuals

toward the highest level of autonomy of which they are capable. Through self-empowerment, individuals become optimistic about life goals.
3. Recovery involves a personal recognition of the need for change and transformation. Individuals must accept that a problem exists and be willing to take steps to address it; these steps usually involve seeking help for a substance use disorder. The process of change can involve physical, emotional, intellectual and spiritual aspects of the person's life.
4. Recovery is holistic. Recovery is a process through which one gradually achieves greater balance of mind, body and spirit in relation to other aspects of one's life, including family, work and community.
5. Recovery has cultural dimensions. Each person's recovery process is unique and impacted by cultural beliefs and traditions. A person's cultural experience often shapes the recovery path that is right for him or her.
6. Recovery exists on a continuum of improved health and wellness. Recovery is not a linear process. It is based on continual growth and improved functioning. It may involve relapse and other setbacks, which are a natural part of the continuum but not inevitable outcomes. Wellness is the result of improved care and balance of mind, body and spirit. It is a product of the recovery process.
7. Recovery emerges from hope and gratitude. Individuals in or seeking recovery often gain hope from those who share their search for or experience of recovery. They see that people can and do overcome the obstacles that confront them and they cultivate gratitude for the opportunities that each day of recovery offers.
8. Recovery involves a process of healing and self-redefinition. Recovery is a holistic healing process in which one develops a positive and meaningful sense of identity.
9. Recovery involves addressing discrimination and transcending shame and stigma. Recovery is a process by which people confront and strive to overcome stigma.
10. Recovery is supported by peers and allies. A common denominator in

the recovery process is the presence and involvement of people who contribute hope and support and suggest strategies and resources for change. Peers, as well as family members and other allies, form vital support networks for people in recovery. Providing service to others and experiencing mutual healing help create a community of support among those in recovery.

11. Recovery involves (re)joining and (re)building a life in the community. Recovery involves a process of building or rebuilding what a person has lost or never had due to his or her condition and its consequences. Recovery involves creating a life within the limitation imposed by that condition. Recovery is building or rebuilding healthy family, social and personal relationships. Those in recovery often achieve improvements in the quality of their life, such as obtaining education, employment and housing. They also increasingly become involved in constructive roles in the community through helping others, productive acts and other contributions.

12. Recovery is a reality. It can, will, and does happen.

Source: CSAT White Paper: Guiding Principles and Elements of Recovery-Oriented Systems of Care.

About the Author

Renée Jones advocates strongly for recognition of issues related to chemical dependency, mental health, prevention and domestic violence. Renée received an award for outstanding leadership and volunteering from the Mental Health Association of Central Alabama in 2004. Mayor Bernard Kincaid of Birmingham Alabama through a City of Birmingham Resolution also recognized Renée's work.

She is a member of NAACP Cleveland Chapter, Counseling & Treating People of Colour, an International Perspective, a conference that draws people from the U.S., Bermuda, Africa, Asia, Europe and the Caribbean, including Puerto Rico, and by National Black Alcoholism & Addiction (BAI). Renée is a nationally- and internationally-known speaker.

Renée is the founder of Reconnection to Life, Inc. (a non-profit organization founded in Birmingham, Alabama from 2001 to 2006). Renee Jones is a woman of great strength & courage. Renee is an author of her first book to be released soon (MAMA AIN'T TEACH ME THAT). Renee is now working on completing her degree. Renee's greatest success is a drug-free life since February 14, 2000.

She is a successful survivor of abuse for eleven years. She did not graduate from high school. Her reading was not good. She spent many years fighting to survive. She stole and sold her soul to the devil. Then in 2001, she found a BIG surprise waiting for her. She found her second life, a life that gave her a chance to enjoy the green earth that God made. February 14, 2000 was the best day of her life. That was the day she stopped using drugs, stopped selling her soul, stopped letting men beat on her, and most of all, was able to say NO and mean NO to rape.

Now, only by the grace of GOD, Renée is CEO of a non-profit organization that supports women recovering from abuse.

This is Renée's first book. At the age of 50, she is mother of three sons with six grandchildren and is ready to live her life.

Let no man pull you low enough to hate him.
Martin Luther King Jr.

www.ingramcontent.com/pod-product-compliance
Lightning Source LLC
Chambersburg PA
CBHW032018040426
42448CB00006B/654